CHRISTIAN
BELIEFS

STUDY GUIDE

CHRISTIAN
BELIEFS

STUDY GUIDE

**Review and Reflection
Exercises on Twenty Basics
Every Christian Should Know**

Wayne Grudem

ZONDERVAN
ACADEMIC

ZONDERVAN ACADEMIC

Christian Beliefs Study Guide
Copyright © 2022 by Wayne Grudem

Requests for information should be addressed to:
Zondervan, *3900 Sparks Dr. SE, Grand Rapids, Michigan 49546*

Zondervan titles may be purchased in bulk for educational, business, fundraising, or sales promotional use. For information, please email SpecialMarkets@Zondervan .com.

ISBN 978-0-310-13620-0 (softcover)

ISBN 978-0-310-13621-7 (ebook)

This study guide was compiled and organized by Peachtree, Inc.

Any internet addresses (websites, blogs, etc.) and telephone numbers in this book are offered as a resource. They are not intended in any way to be or imply an endorsement by Zondervan, nor does Zondervan vouch for the content of these sites and numbers for the life of this book.

Cover design: Rick Szuecs Design
Cover photo: Cristiano de Assuncao / Unsplash
Interior design: Kait Lamphere

Printed in the United States of America

23 24 25 26 27 28 29 30 /TRM/ 14 13 12 11 10 9 8 7 6 5 4 3 2

CONTENTS

Introduction

HOW TO USE THIS STUDY GUIDE

The *Christian Beliefs Study Guide* serves as a companion to the revised and updated edition of *Christian Beliefs*. This guide is designed to help individuals and small groups reflect more deeply on the content in the book and gain a better understanding of Scripture, God, and the Christian life.

The twenty chapters in this study guide correspond to the twenty chapters in *Christian Beliefs*. The study guide includes summaries of the chapters in the book, definitions of key terms, central Scripture passages that relate to the topics in the book, and key quotes from the book. In addition, two types of questions are included in each chapter of the study guide: (1) content questions, which can be answered by reading the chapter, and (2) practical application questions, which encourage reflection and action. This study guide also points readers to my book *Systematic Theology*, second edition, where they can read more about each topic covered in *Christian Beliefs*.

This study guide can be used individually or with a small

group. Small groups who work through the study guide can choose to meet twenty times (one time for each chapter of *Christian Beliefs*) or ten times (two chapters per week). It's up to you and the specific needs of your group.

I hope that this study guide will help you to understand more deeply the material in *Christian Beliefs* and also to discover new ways in which these beliefs can benefit your Christian life.

Wayne Grudem

WHAT IS THE BIBLE?

Chapter Summary

The entirety of the Bible—the Old Testament and the New Testament—is the basis for Christian belief. Every Christian should ask the question, "What is the Bible?" and spend time finding out what God says about his Word within Scripture. This first chapter in *Christian Beliefs* discusses four essential characteristics of the Word of God: its authority, its clarity, its necessity, and its sufficiency. Because Scripture is the words of God, we must spend our lives seeking to understand Scripture if we want to know, trust, and obey God.

Key Terms

evangelical: holding the beliefs that the human words of the Bible are also God's very words to us and that eternal salvation comes only through personal faith in Jesus Christ

1

general revelation: knowledge of God's existence, character, and moral law that is given to all people

special revelation: God's word revealed or spoken to specific people, especially in and through the Bible

Central Scripture Passages

All Scripture is breathed out by God and profitable for teaching, for reproof, for correction, and for training in righteousness, that the man of God may be complete, equipped for every good work.

—*2 Timothy 3:16–17*

Faith comes from hearing, and hearing through the word of Christ.

—*Romans 10:17*

Key Quotes

We are to seek to trust the words of Scripture, for in doing so, we are seeking to trust God himself. And we are to seek to obey the words of Scripture, for in doing so, we are seeking to obey God himself (p. 5).

The Christian life not only starts with the Bible but also thrives through the Bible (p. 9).

Content Questions

1. Does the Bible definitively answer every question we bring to it? Why or why not?

2. Why is it important that the Bible be the basis for our beliefs?

3. How are Christians convicted by the words of the Bible?

4. Why do new scientific or historical facts not contradict Scripture?

Practical Application Questions

1. What is one issue that the Bible speaks clearly on? What is one issue that the Bible does not speak clearly on? How does this affect the emphasis you should place on these issues?

2. In what ways has the Holy Spirit convicted you, guided you, or helped you understand the character of God through the words of Scripture?

3. How do you approach passages in Scripture that are difficult for you to understand? What steps can you take to begin to understand a particular passage of Scripture?

4. Our obedience to God's Word "increases our fellowship with the Holy Spirit and our understanding of the Bible" (p. 8). How have you experienced this personally?

5. How can this chapter help you respond to people who argue that the Bible is not true or that it is full of contradictions?

For Further Reading

To read more about the Bible and what it is, check out the following chapters in Wayne Grudem's *Systematic Theology,* second edition.

Chapter 2: The Word of God
Chapter 3: The Canon of Scripture
Chapter 4: The Four Characteristics of Scripture: (1) Authority
Chapter 5: The Inerrancy of Scripture
Chapter 6: The Four Characteristics of Scripture: (2) Clarity
Chapter 7: The Four Characteristics of Scripture: (3) Necessity
Chapter 8: The Four Characteristics of Scripture: (4) Sufficiency

chapter

WHAT IS GOD LIKE?

Chapter Summary

Because the Bible provides insight into God's existence and his character, any study of God must start by looking at the Bible to see what God has revealed about himself. Each of God's attributes—such as his perfection, holiness, wisdom, omniscience, or justice—demonstrates an aspect of his character and provides us with a perspective on who he is. Learning about God's attributes can also help us understand who he has made us to be. God wants the people he created to know him and to glorify him by reflecting his attributes in their own lives.

Key Terms

omnipotent: possessing infinite power

omnipresent: being unlimited with regard to space; without size or spatial dimensions; present in every point of space with one's whole being

omniscient: knowing all things that exist and all that happens; fully aware at all times of everything, including everything that will happen

Central Scripture Passages

"You shall be holy, for I the LORD your God am holy."

—*Leviticus 19:2*

"I am the Alpha and the Omega," says the Lord God, "who is and who was and who is to come, the Almighty."

—*Revelation 1:8*

Key Quotes

All persons everywhere have a deep, inner sense that God exists, that they are his creatures and that he is their Creator (p. 14).

Every created thing gives evidence of God and his character. But human beings—created in the image of God—give the most evidence of God's existence and character (p. 15).

Content Questions

1. What are some attributes that God most clearly shares with us? What are some attributes he doesn't share very much with us?

2. How is God unchangeable? What parts of the Bible seem to contradict his unchangeableness? How do we reconcile this apparent contradiction?

3. Why is it impossible for God to be limited by material space?

4. What does it mean that God is "jealous"? Why is it not wrong for God to seek his own honor?

Practical Application Questions

1. Name one attribute of God that you would like to imitate more fully in your daily life, and tell why.

2. Think of some of the ways humans are like God. What do they help you understand about yourself or about God?

3. What might some of the dangers be in considering one of God's attributes more important than all the others?

4. Which of God's attributes seems most amazing to you? What have you learned about God through this attribute?

For Further Reading

To read more about God, check out the following chapters in Wayne Grudem's *Systematic Theology*, second edition.

Chapter 9: The Existence of God

Chapter 10: The Knowability of God

Chapter 11: The Character of God: "Incommunicable" Attributes

Chapter 12: The Character of God: "Communicable" Attributes (Part 1)

Chapter 13: The Character of God: "Communicable" Attributes (Part 2)

chapter

WHAT IS THE TRINITY?

Chapter Summary

The idea of the Trinity—one God in three persons—is affirmed throughout the Bible. Each person of the Trinity not only is fully God but also has distinct roles. These roles distinguish God the Father, God the Son (Jesus), and God the Holy Spirit and show how the members of the Trinity relate to one another and to creation. Unity and diversity exist within the Trinity; this exemplifies how we are to experience human relationships that involve unity and diversity.

Key Terms

doctrine of the Trinity: the concept that there is one God who eternally exists as three distinct persons—God the Father, God the Son (Jesus), and God the Holy Spirit—and that each person is fully God

Central Scripture Passages

Jesus came and said to them, "All authority in heaven and on earth has been given to me. Go therefore and make disciples of all nations, baptizing them in the name of the Father and of the Son and of the Holy Spirit."

—Matthew 28:18–19

Building yourselves up in your most holy faith and praying in the Holy Spirit, keep yourselves in the love of God, waiting for the mercy of our Lord Jesus Christ that leads to eternal life.

—Jude 20–21

Key Quote

The unity and diversity that exists in this world is simply a reflection of the unity and diversity that exists within the Trinity (p. 39).

Content Questions

1. Can you name three or four key passages of Scripture that tell us about the Trinity? What exactly do these passages tell us about the Trinity?

2. Why do all analogies fail in their ability to fully explain the Trinity? Does this mean we should try to come up with an analogy that works? Why or why not?

3. What role did each member of the Trinity carry out in creation?

4. How are the different roles within the Trinity seen in our salvation?

Practical Application Questions

1. How do the different ways the Father, Son, and Holy Spirit relate to each other provide us with a model for the ways we are to relate to each other?

2. In which of your relationships are unity and diversity needed for the relationship to grow and deepen?

3. How has learning about the members of the Trinity helped you grow in your faith?

4. Which member of the Trinity do you want to learn more about? What steps will you take to do so?

For Further Reading

To read more about the Trinity, check out the following chapter in Wayne Grudem's *Systematic Theology*, second edition.

Chapter 14: God in Three Persons: The Trinity

4

WHAT IS CREATION?

Chapter Summary

When learning from the Bible about creation, it's important to seek an understanding of how God created the universe, how we should think about and relate to his creation,
how we should respond to our Creator for his work, and
how we should live in light of the truths we know about
creation. This chapter takes a deeper look into the process of creation, the purpose of creation, and our approach
to creation.

Key Terms

[no key terms for this chapter]

Central Scripture Passages

In him we live and move and have our being.

—*Acts 17:28*

By him all things were created, in heaven and on earth, visible and invisible, whether thrones or dominions or rulers or authorities—all things were created through him and for him.

—*Colossians 1:16*

Key Quote

Even a brief reflection on the complexity, diversity, and beauty in creation should cause us to praise God for his power, wisdom, and understanding (p. 43).

Content Questions

1. In what ways do God's acts of creation give us great humility? How do they give us great dignity?

2. What does God think about all of his creation? How did his view of the creation change after Adam and Eve sinned?

3. What is the relationship between science and Scripture? Can they be compatible? Why or why not?

4. In light of God's work of creation, why is nothing but God worthy of our worship?

Practical Application Questions

1. List some of the ways the earth, the animals, and you yourself can give glory to God the Creator.

2. How is God's view of all his creation different from your view of specific aspects of his creation?

3. How can understanding God's involvement in creation help you live life with less fear and more gratefulness?

4. What creative activities do you delight in? How does your participation in these activities give you a greater appreciation for your Creator?

For Further Reading

To read more about creation, check out the following chapters in Wayne Grudem's *Systematic Theology*, second edition.

Chapter 15: Creation
Chapter 21: The Creation of Man

chapter

WHAT IS PRAYER?

Chapter Summary

Our Creator has given us the gift of prayer, which allows us to communicate with him. Our trust in God, our love for him, and our relationship with him can be strengthened through prayer. This chapter highlights the reason for prayer, the effectiveness of prayer, and the proper attitude in prayer.

Key Terms

prayer: personal communication from us to God

Central Scripture Passages

Whatever you ask in prayer, you will receive, if you have faith.

—*Matthew 21:22*

This is the confidence that we have toward him, that if we ask anything according to his will he hears us.

—*1 John 5:14*

Key Quotes

God wants us to pray because it allows us to be a part of a story that is greater than our own (p. 46).

If God only answered the prayers of perfect, sinless people, then God would only answer the prayers of Jesus (p. 49).

Content Questions

1. Is God required to give us what we ask for in prayer? Why or why not?

2. What is the proper attitude we should have when we pray?

3. What hinders our prayers? How do we deal with the things that hinder our prayers?

4. What does it mean to pray "in Jesus' name"?

Practical Application Questions

1. Why does God want us to pray? How have you recently experienced these benefits of prayer? Take a moment to pray, thanking God for how he has blessed you through prayer.

2. Is there anything in your life right now that might be hindering your prayers? If so, take a moment to pray, asking God to forgive you of those things that hinder your prayers.

3. How has your love for and understanding of God deepened through prayer?

4. Have you said any prayers that God has not yet answered? How have you struggled with unanswered prayer? How has your faith grown as a result of unanswered prayer?

For Further Reading

To read more about prayer, check out the following chapters in Wayne Grudem's *Systematic Theology*, second edition.

Chapter 18: Prayer

chapter **6**

WHAT ARE ANGELS, SATAN, AND DEMONS?

───── Chapter Summary ─────

God has created everything in the physical and spiritual realms. Angels, Satan, and demons are real, even if we can't see them. This chapter explains the existence and roles of angels and demons and offers encouragement to Christians. We have no need to fear the attacks of Satan or his demons. Instead, we can trust confidently in Jesus, whose death has already secured victory over evil.

───── Key Terms ─────

angel: a created spiritual being with moral judgment and high intelligence but without a physical body

demon: an evil angel who sinned against God and who now
continually works evil in the world

Central Scripture Passages

"You are the LORD, you alone. You have made heaven,
the heaven of heavens, with all their host, the earth
and all that is on it, the seas and all that is in them;
and you preserve all of them; and the host of heaven
worships you."

—Nehemiah 9:6

God did not spare angels when they sinned, but
cast them into hell and committed them to chains
of gloomy darkness to be kept until the judgment.

—2 Peter 2:4

Key Quotes

We are to worship God and pray to God; we are not to treat
angels, which are part of God's creation, the same way we
would treat God (p. 52).

Someday Christ will come and completely remove the influence of Satan and demons from this world (p. 55).

Content Questions

1. How are the angels like us? How are they different from us?

2. What is the primary role of angels in the world today?

3. What is the primary role of demons in the world today? What tactics do Satan and his demons use to hide the truth of the gospel from people or to hinder a Christian's witness?

4. Who or what is responsible for the evil in the world? What instruction does God's Word give us about how we should handle attacks from Satan and his demons?

Practical Application Questions

1. What are some of the things that the Bible tells us about Satan? How do these things put you on guard against Satan? How do these things remove some fears you may have about Satan?

2. What new insight or understanding have you gained about the spiritual realm from reading this chapter?

3. Are you fighting a spiritual battle now, and if so, how? What steps can you take to tell others the good news of the gospel?

4. In what ways have you experienced spiritual battles? When have you had victory over the influence of evil in your life?

For Further Reading

To read more about angels, Satan, and demons, check out the following chapters in Wayne Grudem's *Systematic Theology*, second edition.

Chapter 19: Angels
Chapter 20: Satan and Demons
Chapter 56: The Final Judgment and Eternal Punishment

chapter

WHAT IS MAN?

=== **Chapter Summary** ===

God created man in his own image for his own glory. This chapter explains the purpose of man, what it means to be created in the image of God, and the responsibilities of God's image bearers. Knowing we were created by God to honor him, represent him, and care for his creation will give us joy and bring meaning to our lives.

=== **Key Terms** ===

[no key terms in this chapter]

Central Scripture Passage

God created man in his own image,
in the image of God he created him;
male and female he created them.
—*Genesis 1:27*

Key Quotes

In Jesus we see God's likeness as it was intended to be. And because of Jesus, we will eventually be changed to reflect God's image as we were intended to do (p. 58).

As God's image bearers—as representatives of the King of the universe—we have the awesome responsibility to help restore his people and his land to the way they were meant to be (p. 59).

Content Questions

1. Why were we created? What are some specific examples of ways we can fulfill the purpose we were created for?

2. What does it mean to be created in God's image?

3. What are our responsibilities as God's image bearers?

Practical Application Questions

1. How does knowing humans are created in God's image affect your view of yourself? How does it affect your view and treatment of other people?

2. What are some ways you and members of your church can fulfill your responsibilities as God's image bearers?

3. How do you give God glory? How does your life show that you are a representative of the King of the universe?

4. What can you do to encourage other people to demonstrate care for God's earth and show respect for the Creator?

For Further Reading

To read more about humankind, check out the following chapters in Wayne Grudem's *Systematic Theology*, second edition.

Chapter 21: The Creation of Man
Chapter 22: Man as Male and Female
Chapter 23: The Essential Nature of Man

chapter

WHAT IS SIN?

=== Chapter Summary ===

Sin existed before Adam and Eve disobeyed God by eating of the Tree of the Knowledge of Good and Evil. But because the first humans sinned, all humans receive a sinful nature that opposes God's perfect nature. This chapter explains what sin is, where sin came from, how God views sin, how sin affects us, and what happens when a Christian sins.

=== Key Term ===

sin: any failure to conform to the moral law of God in act, attitude, or nature

Central Scripture Passages

All have sinned and fall short of the glory of God.

—*Romans 3:23*

As one trespass led to condemnation for all men, so one act of righteousness leads to justification and life for all men. For as by the one man's disobedience the many were made sinners, so by the one man's obedience the many will be made righteous.

—*Romans 5:18–19*

Key Quotes

Sin mars the image of God in us; we no longer reflect the perfection God created us to reflect (p. 61).

Through Jesus' life, death, and resurrection, God offers us freedom from the condemnation sin brings (p. 65).

Content Questions

1. What is sin? How does it affect our lives and the world we live in?

2. How did sin enter the world? Why does God hate sin?

3. Will Christians continue to sin? Why or why not?

4. What are some of the negative results of sin in the life of a Christian? What should Christians do if they sin?

Practical Application Questions

1. How was sin defeated? How does this make you feel? Take a moment to pray, telling God how his defeat of sin makes you feel.

2. How has sin affected your relationship with God? How has it affected your relationships with other people?

3. According to your understanding of sin and man's sinful nature, how do you respond to people who claim that all people are good when they're born?

4. How do you live knowing that Christ, in his death, paid the penalty for your sins—your past, present, and future sins? Who in your life needs to hear the good news of the gospel today?

For Further Reading

To read more about sin, check out the following chapters in Wayne Grudem's *Systematic Theology*, second edition.

Chapter 23: The Essential Nature of Man
Chapter 24: Sin
Chapter 25: The Covenants between God and Man

chapter

WHO IS CHRIST?

Chapter Summary

The eternal Son of God came to earth in the man Jesus Christ, yet he remained fully God. This chapter describes different aspects of Jesus' humanity and shows us why Jesus needed to be both fully God and fully human to save us from the penalty of our sin.

Key Terms

[no key terms for this chapter]

Central Scripture Passages

In him the whole fullness of deity dwells bodily.

—Colossians 2:9

God has highly exalted him and bestowed on him the
name that is above every name, so that at the name
of Jesus every knee should bow, in heaven and on
earth and under the earth, and every tongue confess
that Jesus Christ is Lord, to the glory of God the Father.

—Philippians 2:9–11

Key Quote

The eternal Son of God took to himself a truly human nature.
His divine and human natures are forever distinct and retain
their own properties even though they are eternally and
inseparably united together in one person (p. 71).

Content Questions

1. Why did Jesus have to be fully human when he came to
earth to live and die?

2. What examples are given in the chapter that show evidence of Jesus' humanity?

3. Why did religious leaders want to kill Jesus?

Practical Application Questions

1. Jesus is fully God. What are some ways that this encourages you?

2. Jesus is fully man. What are some ways that this encourages you?

3. Take a moment to pray and talk directly to Jesus, thanking him for coming to earth and becoming fully man for your sake.

4. Hebrews 4:15 tells us that because of Jesus' humanity, he is able to "sympathize with our weaknesses" and that he suffered temptation as we do. How do you respond to these truths about Jesus?

For Further Reading

To read more about Jesus Christ, check out the following chapters in Wayne Grudem's *Systematic Theology*, second edition.

Chapter 26: The Person of Christ
Chapter 29: The Offices of Christ

chapter

WHAT IS THE ATONEMENT?

Chapter Summary

Jesus lived a sinless life and willingly died on the cross to save people from their sins. This chapter describes Jesus' work of atonement on our behalf and highlights the physical and spiritual suffering Jesus experienced so we can be free from the bondage of sin. It explains God's love and justice as the cause of the atonement, why the atonement was necessary, the nature of the atonement, and the result of the atonement.

Key Terms

atonement: the work Jesus did in living and dying to earn our salvation

propitiation: a sacrifice that bears God's wrath toward sin

Central Scripture Passages

God so loved the world, that he gave his only Son, that whoever believes in him should not perish but have eternal life.

—*John 3:16*

He himself bore our sins in his body on the tree, that we might die to sin and live to righteousness. By his wounds you have been healed.

—*1 Peter 2:24*

Key Quotes

Christ came to earn our salvation because of God's faithful love (or mercy) and justice (p. 73).

Christ necessarily and willingly bore the full punishment for our sin on the cross. And so through his death, God's justice was met (p. 77).

Content Questions

1. Why was it necessary for Jesus to come and live a perfect life on earth?

2. Why was it necessary that Jesus die? Could he have saved us in some other way?

3. Why were the sacrifices offered for sins in the Old Testament insufficient to save people from the penalty of their sin?

4. In what way did God's justice and love contribute to his saving us through Jesus' death on the cross?

Practical Application Questions

1. How does your understanding of the atonement humble you? How does it encourage you?

2. Jesus suffered unimaginable physical and spiritual pain as he bore the guilt of our sins. How have you responded to what Jesus has suffered in your place?

3. Have you told other people about what God has done for you through Jesus? If so, how do you go about telling them? If not, what is keeping you from sharing the good news with people?

For Further Reading

To read more about the atonement, check out the following chapters in Wayne Grudem's *Systematic Theology*, second edition.

Chapter 27: The Atonement

WHAT IS THE RESURRECTION?

Chapter Summary

The New Testament is filled with evidence of Jesus' resurrection. This chapter provides examples of this evidence and gives details about Jesus' resurrected body. It highlights the new future life that awaits all who trust in Jesus for their salvation. The chapter ends with a description of Jesus' ascension, when he departed earth for heaven. Christ's life provides a pattern for ours. Just as his resurrection lets us know what will eventually happen to us, his ascension lets us know where we will eventually go.

Key Terms

resurrection: a dead person becoming alive again but with a perfectly renewed physical body that will never again weaken or become old or die

ascension: the lifting up of Jesus from the earth and bringing him into the presence of God in heaven

Central Scripture Passages

He who raised the Lord Jesus will raise us also with Jesus and bring us . . . into his presence.

—*2 Corinthians 4:14*

Blessed be the God and Father of our Lord Jesus Christ! According to his great mercy, he has caused us to be born again to a living hope through the resurrection of Jesus Christ from the dead.

—*1 Peter 1:3*

Key Quotes

Christ earned for us a new future life that is like his own. Although our bodies are not yet like his new body, our spirits have already been made alive with new resurrection power (p. 80).

At the final resurrection, our resurrection, we will receive a new body just like the one Jesus now inhabits (p. 81).

Content Questions

1. Describe Jesus' physical body after his resurrection. How was it different from his body before his death and resurrection? How was it the same?

2. What does resurrection power enable Christians to do?

3. Why did Jesus "not need to remain dead any longer" (p. 81)? What did his death and resurrection accomplish for us?

4. In what ways is Christ's life a pattern for the lives of Christians?

Practical Application Questions

1. Why is it important that Jesus rose from the dead? What would your life be like if he had not risen from the dead?

2. What are some results in your life, and in the whole world, of Jesus' resurrection from the dead?

3. How has your spirit been made alive with Jesus' resurrection power? What does this look like in your life and
in your interactions with other people?

4. What about Jesus' resurrection makes you long for your
own resurrection?

For Further Reading

To read more about the resurrection of Jesus, check out the
following chapters in Wayne Grudem's *Systematic Theology*,
second edition.

Chapter 28: Resurrection and Ascension

chapter

WHAT IS ELECTION?

Chapter Summary

The doctrine of election teaches that God ordained before-hand who will be saved and that not everyone will be saved. This chapter points us to New Testament passages that affirm the doctrine of election and replies to arguments against the doctrine of election. Election ultimately demonstrates God's justice and grace. Because we can do nothing to merit God's grace, all the glory is due God for our salvation.

Key Terms

common grace: a manifestation of God's grace that is common to all people and is different from God's saving grace; a doctrine that teaches that God gives all human beings innumerable blessings in this life that are not part of salvation

election: an act of God, before creation, in which he chooses some people to be saved, not on account of any foreseen merit in them but only because of his sovereign good pleasure

Central Scripture Passages

Those whom he foreknew he also predestined to be conformed to the image of his Son, in order that he might be the firstborn among many brothers.
—*Romans 8:29*

Blessed be the God and Father of our Lord Jesus Christ, who has blessed us in Christ with every spiritual blessing in the heavenly places, even as he chose us in him before the foundation of the world.
—*Ephesians 1:3–4*

Key Quote

The doctrine of election demonstrates to us that God loved us, not for who we are or what we have done or will do, but simply because he decided to love us (p. 94).

Content Questions

1. In light of the doctrine of election, in what ways do our choices have meaning?

2. Why is the doctrine of election so controversial? What are some of the arguments against it?

3. How does the doctrine of election comfort those who believe in Jesus?

4. Why is the work of evangelism still important, even for those who believe the doctrine of election?

Practical Application Questions

1. How does your understanding of the doctrine of election cause you to rejoice? What troubles you about it?

2. Can you name some specific ways in which you have recently seen God bless his creation through common grace? Take a moment to pray, thanking God for specific examples of the grace he has given to all people.

3. Have you struggled to understand the difference between *fairness* and *justice*? How has this chapter helped you better understand the meaning of *justice* and how it's used in relation to God?

4. How does your understanding of the doctrine of election affect your relationship with God? How does it influence your view of people who have chosen not to accept Christ as their Savior?

For Further Reading

To read more about election, check out the following chapters in Wayne Grudem's *Systematic Theology*, second edition.

Chapter 31: Common Grace
Chapter 32: Election and Reprobation

chapter

WHAT DOES IT MEAN TO BECOME A CHRISTIAN?

Chapter Summary

This chapter identifies the blessings of salvation and the order in which they occur in the life of a believer. It describes how people are introduced to the gospel, how they receive the gospel, and the heart change that occurs in those who respond positively to the gospel by placing their trust in Christ for salvation. Highlighted in this chapter are the elements of the gospel call: when sharing the gospel with others, Christians should explain the facts of salvation, invite people to respond in repentance and faith, and share God's promise of forgiveness and eternal life.

Key Terms

conversion: the willing, personal, individual response to the gospel call, in which a person sincerely repents of his sins and places his trust in Christ for salvation

effective calling: an act of God the Father, speaking through the human proclamation of the gospel, in which he summons people to himself in such a way that they respond in saving faith

general calling: the gospel call that goes forth to all people through the human preaching of the gospel

regeneration: a change in an individual's heart before he or she is able to respond in faith to the gospel; a secret act of God in which he imparts new spiritual life to us

Central Scripture Passages

Those whom he predestined he also called, and those whom he called he also justified, and those whom he justified he also glorified.
—*Romans 8:30*

If anyone is in Christ, he is a new creation. The old has passed away; behold, the new has come.
—*2 Corinthians 5:17*

Key Quotes

Once God has summoned through an effective call and changed a person's heart through regeneration, the necessary response is repentance and faith (p. 99).

The job of believers is to explain the gospel message; It is God's job to make that message or call effective (pp. 97–98).

Content Questions

1. How does someone become a Christian?

2. What is the difference between an effective calling and a general calling (or a gospel call)?

3. Can you explain what it means to truly believe in Jesus? What does it mean to truly repent of sins?

4. How are repentance and faith connected?

Practical Application Questions

1. In what ways can Christians give evidence of their belief in Jesus?

2. If you are a Christian, how does your life show evidence of a regenerated heart?

3. How are you telling people the gospel? What steps can you take to make this more of a priority in your life?

4. Why is repentance something Christians need to practice throughout their lives? When have you practiced repentance, and how did it affect you?

For Further Reading

To read more about what it means to be a Christian, check
out the following chapters in Wayne Grudem's *Systematic
Theology*, second edition.

Chapter 33: The Gospel Call and Effective Calling
Chapter 34: Regeneration
Chapter 35: Conversion (Faith and Repentance)

chapter

WHAT ARE JUSTIFICATION AND ADOPTION?

================= Chapter Summary =================

After someone responds to God's call by repenting of their sin and placing their faith in Jesus, God justifies the person and declares the person righteous. God then makes the person a member of his family. All who receive Christ are given the privilege of becoming a child of God. This chapter defines the terms *justification* and *adoption* and helps us gain a deeper understanding of how we are saved through faith and the blessings we receive from God as a result of our faith in Christ.

================= Key Terms =================

adoption: God's act of making those who trust in Christ members of his family

justification: an instantaneous legal act of God in which he (1) thinks of our sins as forgiven and thinks of Christ's righteousness as belonging to us and therefore (2) declares us to be "just," or morally righteous in his sight

Central Scripture Passages

Since we have been justified by faith, we have peace with God through our Lord Jesus Christ.

—*Romans 5:1*

We know that a person is not justified by works of the law but through faith in Jesus Christ, so we also have believed in Christ Jesus, in order to be justified by faith in Christ and not by works of the law, because by works of the law no one will be justified.

—*Galatians 2:16*

Key Quotes

Paul is clear that this justification comes *after* we respond to the gospel call in faith and that justification is God's response to our faith (p. 103).

Because of Christ's work on our behalf, God can, through justification, consider our sins as fully forgiven and consider us as fully acceptable and righteous in his sight (p. 104).

Content Questions

1. What does it mean to be justified? How are Christians justified?

2. Justification is never based on any merit in our faith. Why is this good news for Christians?

3. How do Protestants and Roman Catholics differ in their beliefs surrounding the doctrine of justification?

4. How are justification and adoption linked for someone who has placed their faith in Jesus?

Practical Application Questions

1. If you are a Christian, do you really believe that you have been fully justified once for all time?

2. If you are a Christian, how does it make you feel to be part of God's family? Why does it make you feel this way?

3. How are you encouraged to know that nothing you do can merit your being justified by God?

4. If you have been adopted into God's family, what are some of the blessings and benefits you enjoy as a child of God? What further blessings are you looking forward to when Christ returns?

For Further Reading

To read more about justification and adoption, check out the following chapters in Wayne Grudem's *Systematic Theology*, second edition.

Chapter 36: Justification (Right Legal Standing before God)
Chapter 37: Adoption (Membership in God's Family)

chapter

WHAT ARE SANCTIFICATION AND PERSEVERANCE?

Chapter Summary

Every true Christian goes through a lifelong process of becoming more like Christ. This chapter explains what sanctification is, God's work in sanctification, the believer's role in sanctification, and what it means to persevere through the process. Additionally, this chapter provides scriptural evidence that all true believers will persevere in their faith. The Bible assures us that Jesus' promise of eternal life is for all who believe in him and that the Holy Spirit seals this promise in the life of every Christian.

Key Terms

perseverance of the saints: the two-part teaching that all true Christians will persevere and only those who persevere are true Christians

sanctification: a progressive work of both God and man that makes Christians more and more free from sin and more and more like Christ in their actual lives

Central Scripture Passages

We all, with unveiled face, beholding the glory of the Lord, are being transformed into the same image from one degree of glory to another. For this comes from the Lord who is the Spirit.

—*2 Corinthians 3:18*

You, who once were alienated . . . , he has now reconciled in his body of flesh by his death, in order to present you holy and blameless and above reproach before him, if indeed you continue in the faith, stable and steadfast, not shifting from the hope of the gospel that you heard.

—*Colossians 1:21–23*

Key Quotes

It is important that we continue to grow both in our passive trust in God to sanctify us and in our active striving for holiness and obedience in our lives (p. 111).

Sanctification is a lifelong process (p. 116).

Content Questions

1. How is sanctification different from justification?

2. What is our role in sanctification? What is God's role?

3. What does Jesus promise to all who persevere in their faith in him?

4. How are Christians assured that their salvation is genuine?

Practical Application Questions

1. What are some specific ways in which you could contribute more to your sanctification in the coming week?

2. List some passages of Scripture that support the doctrine of perseverance. As you reflect on those passages, how do they make you feel? Why do they make you feel that way?

3. What evidence in your life gives you assurance of your salvation and your perseverance in your faith?

4. The apostle Paul wrote, "Sin will have no dominion over you, since you are not under law but under grace" (Rom. 6:14). How are you encouraged by these words as they relate to your sanctification?

For Further Reading

To read more about sanctification and perseverance, check out the following chapters in Wayne Grudem's *Systematic Theology*, second edition.

Chapter 38: Sanctification (Growth in Likeness to Christ)
Chapter 39: Baptism in and Filling with the Holy Spirit
Chapter 40: The Perseverance of the Saints
     (Remaining a Christian)

chapter

WHAT IS DEATH?

Chapter Summary

For the Christian, death is not a punishment. God works through death to complete our sanctification. Because of this, Christians should not fear death. This chapter discusses what happens when a Christian dies, what happens when a non-Christian dies, why death exists, how God works good through hardships and death, and what happens to our bodies when Christ returns.

Key Terms

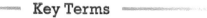

glorification: the process by which believers in Jesus will receive renewed resurrection bodies just like their Savior

resurrection bodies: new, imperishable bodies that will not wear out, grow old, or ever be subject to sickness or disease

Central Scripture Passages

I do not account my life of any value nor as precious to myself, if only I may finish my course and the ministry that I received from the Lord Jesus, to testify to the gospel of the grace of God.

—*Acts 20:24*

Yes, we are of good courage, and we would rather be away from the body and at home with the Lord.

—*2 Corinthians 5:8*

Key Quote

God uses the experience of death to complete our sanctification. God uses death as a means to make us more like Christ (p. 119).

Content Questions

1. Why do Christians die?

2. What happens to the bodies and what happens to the souls of Christians when they die?

3. What will happen to the bodies of Christians when Jesus returns to earth?

Practical Application Questions

1. How does knowing why Christians die affect the way you think about your own death someday?

2. When you think about what happens to the bodies and souls of Christians when they die, how does this make you feel? Why does it make you feel this way?

3. What specific aspects of our resurrection bodies are you especially hopeful about?

4. How has pain or hardship in your life strengthened your faith?

For Further Reading

To read more about life after death, check out the following chapters in Wayne Grudem's *Systematic Theology*, second edition.

Chapter 41: Death and the Intermediate State
Chapter 42: Glorification (Receiving a Resurrection Body)
Chapter 43: Union with Christ

chapter

WHAT IS THE CHURCH?

Chapter Summary

God's church is made up of all true believers in Christ, regardless of what time period they lived in. This chapter describes the nature of the church in general—all believers—and the specific details of local church gatherings. It guides us in determining what makes a church a true church. The chapter also explains God's purpose for his church and highlights the ministry of the church, which is accomplished through worship, nurture, and evangelism and mercy. The Holy Spirit empowers believers with the spiritual gifts necessary to carry out the ministry of the church.

Key Terms

a church: a community of God's people at any level
the church: the community of all true believers for all time

invisible church: the church as God sees it, since only he knows the spiritual condition of people's hearts

sacraments: ordinances of the church—baptism and the Lord's Supper

spiritual gifts: gifts of the Holy Spirit that are required to do the ministry of the church

visible church: the church as Christians on earth see it

Central Scripture Passage

Christ loved the church and gave himself up for her, that he might sanctify her, having cleansed her by the washing of water with the word, so that he might present the church to himself in splendor, without spot or wrinkle or any such thing, that she might be holy and without blemish.

—*Ephesians 5:25–27*

Key Quotes

As members of the church, we should pursue its purity in all areas to the best of our ability (p. 128).

With the full confidence in Christ's promise that he will build his church (Matt. 16:18), every church should wholeheartedly seek to worship God, build its members to maturity, and preach the good news of the gospel to the world through word and deed (p. 129).

Content Questions

1. How is a church different from a Bible study or Christian retreat?

2. What is the difference between the visible church and the invisible church?

3. What are the marks of a true church?

4. God created the church to fulfill three purposes. What are they? What is the Holy Spirit's role in the ministry of the church?

Practical Application Questions

1. Why should Christians become members of a church? What are some dangers of not becoming a member of a local church?

2. Can you list some of the things a church is supposed to do? Can you name some specific examples of the Holy Spirit's work empowering and blessing some of those things in your own church?

3. How should a church pursue purity and unity?

4. What are some ways that church members can use their spiritual gifts to encourage and build up the church?

For Further Reading

To read more about the Christian church, check out the following chapters in Wayne Grudem's *Systematic Theology*, second edition.

Chapter 50: The Lord's Supper

Chapter 51: Worship

Chapter 52: Gifts of the Holy Spirit: (1) General Questions

Chapter 53: Gifts of the Holy Spirit: (2) Specific Gifts

WHAT WILL HAPPEN WHEN CHRIST RETURNS?

Chapter Summary

Jesus promised his followers that he would return. But when is he coming back? While the Bible is clear that no one will know the time of Christ's return, it points to some signs that will precede his coming and provides some details about what will happen in the future. Many debates in the church are related to the return of Christ and the end times, especially surrounding the thousand-year period we read about in Revelation 20. This chapter lays out some of the views regarding the timing of Jesus' return and how it relates to the thousand years.

Key Terms

amillennial view: a view of the millennium as occurring now, and when it ends, Jesus will return

eschatology: studies of future events ("last things")

millennium: a thousand-year period of time

postmillennial view: a view of the millennium as coming gradually, which places Jesus' return after the millennium

premillennial view: a view of the millennium as coming suddenly, which places Jesus' return before the millennium

pretribulational premillennial view: a view of Christ's return that holds that Jesus will return twice: once in a secret return and then seven years later in a second, public return

Central Scripture Passages

"You also must be ready, for the Son of Man is coming at an hour you do not expect."

—*Matthew 24:44*

The Lord himself will descend from heaven with a cry of command, with the voice of an archangel, and with the sound of the trumpet of God. And the dead in Christ will rise first.

—*1 Thessalonians 4:16*

Key Quote

Although no one can know the time of Christ's return, all believers should respond as John did in Revelation 22:20 when he heard Christ say, "Surely I am coming soon." John's response was "Amen. Come, Lord Jesus!" (pp. 132–33).

Content Questions

1. What are some issues relating to eschatology that Christians differ on?

2. What are some of the signs that will occur before the return of Christ? Why is it difficult to know whether any of the signs have already occurred?

3. What are the three views on the millennium? Which view does the Bible seem to support? Why?

Practical Application Questions

1. What are some things about eschatology that all Christians should agree on? Which of those things give you the greatest joy?

2. Take a moment to read Revelation 22:12. How might this verse challenge the way you live? In response, take a moment to pray John's prayer as found in Revelation 22:20.

3. How have the explanations and descriptions in this chapter challenged or supported your views on future events?

4. In light of Scripture, what is your personal view of when Christ will return?

For Further Reading

To read more about the second coming of Christ, check out the following chapters in Wayne Grudem's *Systematic Theology*, second edition.

Chapter 54: The Return of Christ: When and How?
Chapter 55: The Millennium

chapter

WHAT IS THE FINAL JUDGMENT?

Chapter Summary

This chapter helps us better understand the final judgment that will take place after Christ returns. All people will be judged, both Christians and non-Christians. Those who have placed their faith in Christ will be rewarded for the good they have done. Those who have rejected Jesus will receive their punishment—an eternity in hell. Knowing there will be a final judgment should motivate followers of Jesus to tell others about their Savior. The Bible's warnings about the final judgment should encourage non-Christians to repent of sin and place their faith in Jesus.

Key Terms

final judgment: the day God has determined when "he
will judge the world in righteousness" through Christ
(Acts 17:31)

hell: the place of eternal punishment

Central Scripture Passages

God will bring every deed into judgment, with every
secret thing, whether good or evil.

—Ecclesiastes 12:14

"Truly, truly, I say to you, whoever hears my word
and believes him who sent me has eternal life. He
does not come into judgment, but has passed from
death to life."

—John 5:24

Key Quote

The final judgment will take place so that God can display his
glory to all mankind by demonstrating his justice and mercy
simultaneously (p. 145).

Content Questions

1. What happens to Christians at the final judgment? What will happen to those who have rejected Jesus' claims?

2. For believers, how is the final judgment a source of encouragement rather than fear?

3. What does the Bible tell us about hell?

Practical Application Questions

1. How does your understanding of the final judgment affect your life today? How does it affect the way you relate to others?

2. How can thinking about the final judgment help you forgive other people and leave vengeance in God's hands?

3. If you are a believer, does the reality of the final judgment and hell motivate you to tell people about how you have been saved through faith in Christ? What steps can you take this week to share the good news of Jesus with someone who needs to hear it?

4. How does your understanding of hell make you feel? Why does it make you feel that way?

For Further Reading

To read more about the final judgment and hell, check out the following chapters in Wayne Grudem's *Systematic Theology*, second edition.

Chapter 56: The Final Judgment and Eternal Punishment

chapter

WHAT IS HEAVEN?

━━━ **Chapter Summary** ━━━

This final chapter answers some questions about the eternal dwelling place of believers. It defines what heaven is, tells of the renewed heavens and earth that God will create, and describes the joy and fulfillment believers will experience in the presence of God.

━━━ **Key Terms** ━━━

heaven: the place where God dwells and most fully manifests his presence

Central Scripture Passages

The King will say to those on his right, "Come, you who are blessed by my Father, inherit the kingdom prepared for you from the foundation of the world."

—*Matthew 25:34*

I heard a loud voice from the throne saying, "Behold, the dwelling place of God is with man. He will dwell with them, and they will be his people, and God himself will be with them as their God."

—*Revelation 21:3*

Key Quotes

Heaven is the place where God most fully makes known his presence to bless (p. 150).

In addition to being a place of unimaginable beauty, heaven will be a place where God's glory is so undeniably evident that all of creation will function in a way that is in full cooperation with his will (p. 151).

Content Questions

1. How will we interact with and worship God in heaven?

2. How should believers in Jesus live while we await our life in heaven?

3. What will be our greatest joy in heaven?

Practical Application Questions

1. Can you list some of the things the Bible says about heaven?

2. In what ways does the Bible's description of heaven surprise you, encourage you, and make you long for heaven even more?

3. How will human beings be more like God in heaven?

4. Take a moment to pray, thanking God for specific aspects of heaven.

For Further Reading

To read more about the new heavens and the new earth, check out the following chapters in Wayne Grudem's *Systematic Theology*, second edition.

Chapter 57: The New Heavens and New Earth